Becoming the BlueLotus:
A Reiki Level Two Handbook

By Storm Faerywolf

©2010-2011 Storm Faerywolf. All rights reserved. No part of this book may be reproduced or transmitted in any form or by any means, electronic or mechanical, including photocopying, recording or by any information storage and retrieval system, without written permission from the author, except for the inclusion of brief quotations in a review.

This book is designed to provide information on using BlueLotus Reiki. It is presented with the understanding that the publisher and author are not engaged in rendering medical, psychological or legal services and do not prescribe the use of any technique for treatment of medical or psychological problems without the advice of a licensed medical or psychological practitioner.

The intent of the author is to offer information of a general nature to help you in your search for emotional and spiritual well being. The author and publisher shall assume no responsibility for any loss or damage caused, or alleged to have been caused, directly or indirectly, by the information contained in this book.

"The Reiki Principles
The Secret Method of Inviting Blessings
The spiritual Medicine of Many Illnesses...
For today only anger not, worry not...
Be Grateful and humble, do your work with appreciation.
Be kind to all.
In the morning and at night, with hands held in prayer,
Think this in your mind; chant this with your mouth.
The Usui Reiki Method to change your mind and body for the better."

-Mikao Usui

Preface

This book is based on my Reiki Level Two class and is intended first and foremost to be a supplement to the teachings given therein. Since Reiki is not passed as ordinary knowledge and instead as an energetic event, one cannot simply pick up this manual and become a Reiki II practitioner. For this, one must be attuned (aka initiated) to the second level of Reiki by a qualified Reiki Master/Teacher.

One can, however, learn some of the philosophies of our tradition, as well as some meditative and energetic exercises that will enhance their experiential understanding of energy and at the very least prepare them for practicing Reiki should they eventually become attuned to our path.

BlueLotus *is the name that I have given to my practice and school of Reiki. In Eastern thought the lotus represents regeneration and spiritual illumination. It is also a symbol of the ability to transcend the muck (where it is rooted) and grow even through the dirtiest of waters (life experience) and into the pure sunlight of enlightenment (where the flower blooms). The blue lotus also represents wisdom, and to the ancient Egyptians symbolized rebirth, as they saw it close and descend beneath the waters each night, only rise up from the waters the following day. To me this is a perfect symbol for Reiki practice; a practice that promotes enlightenment, wisdom, transformation, and renewal.*

At the end of this book is a list of resources that you may find helpful in your search.

TABLE OF CONTENTS

INTRODUCTION 7
CHAPTER ONE: "Becoming Reiki" 11
CHAPTER TWO: "Additional Techniques, Part 1" 15
CHAPTER THREE: "Using Symbols in Reiki" 19
CHAPTER FOUR: "Mental & Emotional Healing" 43
CHAPTER FIVE: "Distant Healing" 47
CHAPTER SIX: "Additional Techniques, Part 2" 53
CHAPTER SEVEN: "Ethics" 59
CHAPTER EIGHT: "The Professional Practitioner" 67
APPENDIX: Resources 77

Introduction

My personal journey with Reiki began many years ago and is detailed in my book *"Awakening the BlueLotus"*. In it I describe how I first learned of Reiki and how my attunement to Level One left me with a sense of having a better connection to an energy current that I was already in possession of. This is one of the points of Reiki that I think is most often misunderstood; many expect that the attunement will grant them access to energies that they were previously unaware of when in fact it is just the opposite: to be attuned to Reiki is, in one sense, to have reaffirmed that which you already had. Reiki, as a system, is to be a channel for "universal Life-force" and by definition, all living things must already be in possession of this energy. So what then is the point of the attunement?

Even with my Reiki I attunement I knew that something had changed; not the energy that I was in possession of, but something inside of me. Blocks to my own power that I did not even know were there suddenly were brought up to my awareness. Using the spiritual skills at my disposal I worked to clear them away, to transform them, and ultimately, to reclaim that energy as my own, becoming stronger in doing so. The attunement was a catalyst for that awakening and gave me a context by which I could better work with divine energy.

When I received my Reiki II things were a bit different.

First, I experienced almost none of the tangible *bliss* that I had felt with Reiki I. That's fine, I thought, every initiation is different. What I *didn't* realize at the time, however, is that the same process was playing out as before, only now on a different level. My "blocks" were less physical this time around. They were emotional... mental barriers that I had erected for myself without knowing how or why. This became apparent to me when I encountered resistance to learning the material given at Reiki II.

In this level we are taught and attuned to three symbols which have various qualities for focusing the energy being channeled in Reiki, opening up new areas for the work. One of these symbols is rather complicated, a Japanese kanji character with 22 strokes which is used to send Reiki over long distances. While the other symbols were relatively easy to master, I found memorizing this final symbol a daunting task which, in a decidedly "sour grapes" fashion, led me to abandon the formal practices of Reiki all together. It wasn't until years later after I had a series of dreams[1] that I decided to take up my studies again and was finally able to master this symbol.

Even though for those few years I had abandoned the formal practices of Reiki I still was able to reap the benefits that the attunement had afforded me, namely an increased capacity for channeling energy, along with a deepened awareness of how energy moves and its effects on the practitioner and the recipient.

The attunements to Reiki have various effects on the individuals who experience them ranging from increased psychic sensitivity, deeper emotional control and connection to others, accelerated healing, and quickened spiritual growth, to name but a few. Most people report that their capacity for channeling energy is increased with each successive level. In addition to these effects the symbols that are taught at level two begin to affect us in deep ways the more that we use them.

Included in this book are various practices designed to assist the Reiki II practitioner in developing their skills. Many of these

---

[1] For a complete account of this, please see my book *"Awakening the BlueLotus: A Reiki Level One Handbook"*, ©2010 Storm Faerywolf.

exercises have been re-imported to the West from Japan via Western Reiki Masters who had travelled there in search of Reiki's origins[2]. Since I do not claim to have any firsthand knowledge of Japanese language or customs I have taken the liberty of renaming them based on my interpretation of the function of the exercises themselves and not as a direct translation. I have also included the Japanese name for the sake of tradition and respect to the culture. Any errors or misrepresentations given here are completely my own.

This manual also details my own experience and perspectives on the practices of Reiki which are colored by my work outside of this specific tradition. In particular my take on the symbols of Reiki II reflect my work with the Three Souls; the etheric anatomy of the human being as espoused by the practices of Huna and Feri tradition witchcraft. While some might claim that this is "not Reiki" (and indeed this was not something that was taught to me in a Reiki context nor do I believe that the founder held such a view) I would remind the reader that Reiki is not a religion, but a spiritual practice that claims to be able to compliment whatever religion or spiritual practices you are already engaged in. With this in mind I see no problem with including insights gleaned from other spiritual work, and in fact I think it is necessary to the continued development of one's spiritual progression in general and of the living tradition of Reiki in particular. I am not a Buddhist and do not claim to have any special knowledge of Buddhist practice from which Reiki most certainly originated. I am a Westerner, and as such my mind is trained in a much different way than those who grew up in Japan or other Eastern lands where the principles and practices of Buddhism were the norm. I do not see this as a detriment. On the contrary, I see this as an opportunity to combine many different flavors of knowledge and spiritual

---

[2] See *The Spirit of Reiki*, ©2001 Walter Lübeck, Frank Arjava Petter, and William Lee Rand.

practice, the end result being a new perspective with roots in an older tradition, but whose flowers and fruits yield something new. There will be some who disagree with my approach and the conclusions afforded by them. That is wonderful! This means that we are all engaged with our own path, a goal that I very much feel Reiki (and the true spiritual path in general) encourages in each of us.

If you have received a Reiki II attunement then this manual will provide some tools to help you to increase your connection to the energy as well as guide you in furthering your studies with the symbols. If you are considering taking the Reiki II attunement then this book will prepare you for what will come when you finally take the plunge. Either way it is my sincere hope that you will find the practices here useful as you continue on your spiritual path.

Storm Faerywolf
December, 2010

CHAPTER ONE:
Becoming Reiki

The spiritual principles and practices of Reiki were largely lost when imported to the West. In the permutations of the tradition that have evolved in the West since the time of Takata, the emphasis has been on that of physical healing almost to the complete exclusion of the spirituality that is at its heart.

Reiki was originally practiced as a "secular enlightenment & healing system" with practices geared toward openness, acceptance, and a gentle rejection of negative pre-conditioning, seen as the root cause of disharmony and disease.

In Reiki I we are introduced to the concepts of Reiki which give us a particular context of interacting with universal life-force energy. The first attunement "awakens" our own energy centers, making us more aware of this universal energy and – with the meditative and energetic practices– we reach through that new-found awareness to become a channel for this universal force.

The emphasis of this level is that of *doing*; we are taught various techniques. We diligently endeavor to observe these techniques so as to make our connection stronger, clearing out our personal blocks, and generally improving our spiritual practice.

In Reiki II we are encouraged not simply to *do* Reiki, but now to *be* Reiki; to deepen our practice by applying the Principles –not just in the context of a session, but in everyday life. It is at this stage in our development that we are asked to release our false conditioning: anger, fear, worry, doubt. If we have been practicing the Principles with regularity then we will have entered into a state of being that better enables us to live somewhat less entangled by these distractions so that we are able to mindfully respond to a situation, instead of just mindlessly reacting.

This process began the moment we embarked upon this journey; the practices that we have been taught in Reiki I are geared to bring us into the present moment, giving us an opportunity to engage that which heals mind, body, and spirit. This clears our channel for the power, and encourages our energy-body to engage in Reiki more often, giving us more opportunities to clear our own blocks. Being a channel for Reiki causes us to begin our own healing process, and once we can heal our false beliefs and conditioning and move beyond fear then healing flows through us as naturally as our breath. As before, this begins with the Principles.

THE FIVE PRINCIPLES OF REIKI

Just for today, anger not.
Just for today, worry not.
Be grateful.
Work on yourself with appreciation.
Be kind to all living things.

As described in my Level One manual, the Five Principles comprise a sort of spiritual formula that enables us to live in the present moment, free of those ego distractions that keep us *small* and "cut off" from the divine source.

They should be seen less as "commandments" and more as a spiritual exercise. We are not admonished for those times in which we do not apply the Principles, but use them as a means to return to "right thinking" after we have fallen.

When we are able to put the Principles into action, then we are less likely to operate from fear, anger, or worry. What we have done is to effectively relinquish *control*; we simply allow things to be as they naturally are and release the need to change them. In this we begin to embody the concept of *wei-wu-wei*, or "doing by not doing"; an essential state of mind for effectively channeling the presence of Reiki.

Revisiting The Spiritual Practices of Reiki I

It is important to remember what we were taught in the previous level, as the practices of Reiki I form a foundation that is necessary to mastering the material taught in level II. If you are not already proficient in the following techniques then you should perform them every day for the next 30 days in order to prepare for the newer work. (For full descriptions of these practices please see my Reiki I manual, *Awakening the BlueLotus*.)

Gassho Breathing
As in Reiki I we begin with Gassho breathing. This gives us a way of relaxing the mind and body, encouraging both to drift into a state of relaxed *stillness*. Thoughts that arise are acknowledged, and are released. This is an exercise in *the present moment*; a common theme in Reiki and other spiritual pursuits. This is expanded upon with the further practices offered by the Usui Reiki system.

Chanting the Principles
The practice of chanting the Five Principles of Reiki is one that Usui himself recommended to his students as a way to calm the mind and to focus it toward the work to be done. If you have been doing this practice (in the morning upon waking, and at night just before bed, according to Usui) then you will have noticed that they have begun to work upon your consciousness in new ways. If you have not been doing this regularly, then try doing this for the next 30 days and check in with yourself after to see if you notice any differences in how you feel and also in how you might react to outside stimuli.

Waterfall Meditation

This method of connecting to Reiki is deceptively simple and yet provides a clear and strong method for opening up to spiritual energy as well as for clearing the channels of blocks that may impede its flow. With a little imagination it can be expanded to include the conscious direction of Reiki into different areas of the body.

Thought Empowerment #1 (Nentatsu Ho)

In Reiki I we learned the first of the Thought Empowerment techniques, called "Nentatsu ho". This is the process of using Reiki to empower a positive thought or affirmation. Sometimes referred to as the "Habit Technique" or even "Deprogramming", it is a method for transforming negative thought patterns so as to free up wasted personal *ki* as well as empower positive thoughts so that they hold more "weight" than the negative ones we often bombard ourselves with. This can be performed on yourself or for your clients.

•

Make sure to take your time with the above exercises before moving on to the next chapter, especially if you have not already been doing them in relation to your Level One work. While it is true that some Reiki Masters will train and attune individuals and groups to Levels I and II in a single weekend (and even to I, II, and III in such short a time!) I feel that this robs the student from the experience of gentle *unfolding* that occurs when we take our time with the work. There is no substitute for the experience that comes from the practice itself, so do yourself a favor and practice, practice, practice!

CHAPTER TWO:
Additional Techniques, Part 1

Once we have mastered the techniques given in Level One we can begin to include other methods aimed at deepening our Reiki practice. Take your time with the following exercises and keep records of your experiences.

Tanden Breathing

This is a simple technique used to increase your capacity for feeling and channeling energy. This also serves to rejuvenate your own life-force for increased health and vitality. This may be used as a stand-alone exercise or in conjunction with your preferred method of connecting to Reiki prior to any meditation or Reiki session.

Step 1: Connect to Reiki using the Waterfall Meditation.

Step 2: Become aware of the flow of Reiki moving from your heart-center and down into your *tanden*. (This is an energy-center that is usually described as being a point in your body about 1 ½" beneath your navel and 2" behind it.) Feel Reiki energizing this area for the span of at least three breaths.

Step 3: With each breath, imagine the light of Reiki concentrating in your *tanden*, glowing brighter and larger with each inhale until it becomes about the size of a grapefruit. Maintain this sense for several moments as you *feel* the power as being warm and vibrant within you.

Step 4: With a breath, expand this energy to fill the entirety of your physical body. Take another few moments to feel Reiki brimming with you, permeating your entire being.

Step 5: Take another deep breath and on your exhale feel the energy radiating outward from the pores in your skin and out to the edges of the universe into infinity. Feel this expansiveness for at least a few moments.

Step 6: With your inhale, begin to bring this energy back to you concentrating it once more in your *tanden*.

With practice you can achieve a level of proficiency with this exercise in which you can send the power outward to the edges of the universe with every exhale and back to your *tanden* with each inhale making this exercise reminiscent of "psychic crunches". Repeat for as long as desired.

THE MICROCOSMIC ORBIT

The Microcosmic Orbit is an energy exercise imported into Reiki from *Kikou*, a Japanese form of Chinese Qi Gong. It is a means to circulate *ki* through the body so as to increase the charge and to clear out any blockages that may be present in the energy channels of the body.

Creating the flow of energy in the Microcosmic Orbit is simple. Locate the *Hui Yin* (perineum) between the anus and the genitals, a major point of *ki* in the body. *Gently* clenching this point increases the energy in spurts and can be an effective way of kick-starting your own energy. The tongue should be touching the roof of the mouth against the back of the teeth when engaging it. When these two points of *ki* are engaged we can begin the following exercise.

Imagine energy as a golden light entering into your crown, which then proceeds down the front of your body, across the *Hui Yin* toward the back of your body, up the spine through all the chakras, across the crown of the head and through that point where your tongue connects to the roof of your mouth where it enters into the cycle again. Continue to be aware of the flow of energy as it builds in this ever-flowing circular movement. Breathing and moving energy in this manner will help to center the body and raise personal energy prior to a session. Do this up to a few minutes at a time in order to "jump start" your own energy prior to a session, or at any point when you feel you need an extra "boost". It is unnecessary to do this for an entire session, however as doing so may actually encourage your energy-body to use your own life-force as opposed to being simply open to universal energy. Practice with this and see how it feels to you.

THE VIOLET BREATH

The Violet Breath is another exercise imported into Reiki but one that is very useful, especially as a foundation for other exercises that we will explore later.

Imagine a cloud of white light all around you. As you breathe in, gently clench the *Hui Yin* and feel this light enter your microcosmic orbit where it gradually becomes violet. After several breaths (or several minutes of breathing in this way) feel how it gathers in your belly, becoming concentrated. When you feel that you have built up a sufficient charge, exhale forcefully and imagine this violet light shining out on your breath. This may be used in a session in order to remove blocks or to charge up the energy body of the recipient, or it may be used in order to empower the symbols that are used at this level of Reiki.

•

When these exercises become familiar then can we progress to focusing our Reiki practice further with the addition of the Sacred Symbols.

CHAPTER THREE:
USING SYMBOLS IN REIKI

One of the main distinctions between Reiki and most other types of energy healing practice is the use of certain symbols to affect the use of the power. In Reiki II we are attuned to three symbols that allow us to deepen our understanding of spiritual energies, thus increasing our capacity for channeling energy, as well as focusing on specific "vibrations" within the larger spectrum of universal life-force.

These symbols are "keys" that are empowered in the initiate by a Reiki Master during the attunement process; these keys being placed with intent and energetic ceremony into specific areas of the initiate's energy-body for the purpose of "unlocking" or otherwise awakening varying vibrations within the initiate's consciousness. While the first Reiki attunement opened up the initiate's energy-body[3] in such a way so as to "wire" it to channel universal life-force, the second attunement "turns up the volume"; widening one's energy channels or otherwise increasing one's capacity for handling and directing that universal force. This is achieved in part by introducing the sacred symbols, giving the initiate energetic access to them, and thus a means to allow them to change us from within.

The symbols themselves are a language that speaks of the anatomy and progression of the soul. They –along with the Principles and the practices –keep the energy channeled by Reiki

---

[3] I say this really as a form of conversational shorthand for in reality there is no additional "opening up" involved with the attunement as each and every one of us are already "open" to universal life-force (for if we were not we would not be alive). What happens during the attunement is that the initiate is consciously and energetically *reminded* (that is to say, be made consciously aware) of that connection they already possess. It is this consciousness that allows the power to flow and what causes changes to occur within the initiate.

practitioners "safe" for all involved. One of the foundational beliefs of Reiki stemming from Usui is that Reiki can never harm; the very idea of harm being contrary to the essence of what Reiki is. Though it is certainly true that misdirected life-force energy *can* (and often does) cause harm[4], another major distinction of Reiki from other energy healing modalities is the belief that the energy accessed in Reiki is guided by a higher spiritual power which directs it to only where it is *needed*. In this system it is the combination of the practices, the Principles, and the sacred symbols that ensure that this energy is under the guidance of a higher spiritual consciousness. The power involved in Reiki is in fact, divine presence.

The symbols on their own do not convey the essence or power of Reiki. They cannot. For they are merely doorways into an energetic experience that is initiated by the attunement experience, and cultivated by the practice. But unlike some Reiki practitioners I am not quick to dismiss them as being powerless on their own. My feeling is that they are "plugged in" to the powers that they represent and so may be drawn upon to a limited degree even by those who are not attuned to Reiki and still receive some benefit. Those attuned, however, will find that their energetic relationship with them is infinitely stronger because of their formalized energetic relationship with them.

While we may find ourselves content in using the symbols strictly in the context of a formal Reiki session or attunement, the symbols can be interacted with in a multitude of ways, each offering specific changes in our consciousness and energy-field. Once attuned, we have a heightened relationship with these symbols, but with practice and meditation comes a deeper understanding of their energetic language, as well as an

---

[4] "Unchecked, the life force is cancer; unbridled, the death force is war and genocide." Starhawk. *The Spiral Dance: A Rebirth of the Ancient Religion of the Great Goddess.* ©1979. Harper-Collins.

increased capacity for the powers that these symbolic keys unlock.

In American Reiki practice the tradition was an oral one, and much emphasis was placed on the symbols being sacred, secret and available only to the initiated. Because of this many practitioners, both traditional and modern, feel that these symbols should not be disclosed to the uninitiated. Since practitioners have begun to write of the tradition, some Reiki Masters have made the decision to display them openly and so the symbols have been readily available in the form of books and websites so that anyone can see them. Furthermore, the symbols used have their origins in older spiritual systems such as Shintoism and Tendai Buddhism where they are not held as secret, and even the practices of Reiki in Japan they are not considered to be secret. Sacred, yes... secret, no.

Some people keep things as sacred by keeping them secret. It's a powerful technique; if some symbol or ritual or piece of lore is never shared with another (or with those considered to be 'outsiders') then it creates a special type of consciousness which can lend itself to a heightened spiritual relationship with the object of one's (secretive) attention. Emotions connected to the symbol are heightened and become larger players in the internal landscape. This is the basis of many secret societies and initiatory mystery traditions; a shared secret is sacred and thus powerful.

This, however, is but one of many techniques that can be employed in the effort to imbue a symbol with potency. Other approaches with varying degrees of effectiveness include meditation, performing rituals, dancing, singing & chanting, creating works of art, and even simply engaging in deep conversations about them. When our attentions are turned toward the symbols and the powers they unlock, then we are in a sense "fine tuning" our connections to the universal signal that is Reiki.

I was taught that the symbols are akin to "training wheels"; that they serve a purpose in training but eventually may be abandoned as the practitioner becomes more experienced in working with energy. This shouldn't be misinterpreted as to mean that they are unimportant. On the contrary, the symbols are at the very least reminders of the function and purpose of Reiki and as such are sacred whether they are to be used in a session or not. In practical terms, the symbols are used as "triggers", helping us to "tune in" to specific frequencies of the universal life-force. Once we can "tune in" at will we may not need to use them, but this process can take years for some. Many practitioners continue to use them out of respect for tradition and for the simple fact that they work!

I have heard from some Reiki Masters that showing the symbols to those who have yet to be attuned will somehow cause them to be "incorrectly linked to lower vibrational energies" which could then "result in the reduction of the symbols value to the new healer forever." All I can say to this is that this has not been my experience, and I sincerely doubt that anyone holding this belief has any evidence to support this. On the contrary it is common practice in some lineages to specifically show the student the symbols *before* the attunement so that their conscious mind will also participate in the empowerment of the symbols during the attunement process.

I have also heard that merely seeing them will (either fully or partially) attune the viewer. Again this would appear to be based on nothing more than fear of change; for if simply seeing them would attune the individual why the need for a Reiki Master? As nice as it might be for this to be true (who *wouldn't* want millions of Reiki attuned individuals channeling spiritual energies into the world?) all evidence clearly reveals this to be nonsensical. As with all things of a spiritual nature, there is no one right way that we can default to; we must ever be prepared to live in the present moment and allow the energies themselves to inform us lest we descend into mindless dogma.

To those who would look toward the origins of the Reiki tradition for insight into this issue I feel it necessary to point out that many now report that Usui did not consider the symbols to be secret. They were adopted from various other spiritual systems and were commonly displayed in the open. The sacredness held for them was reinforced by the *practice* of Reiki, not one's ability to keep them occulted.

According to Reiki Master Vincent Amador:

> In the western "Traditional" practices the symbols are "secret" and "sacred". In the western "Non-Traditional" practices, it is not uncommon for them to be openly displayed. In Japan, the symbols appear to be somewhat common and have been observed to be written on all sorts of objects in public view. They are also a part of traditional Buddhist practice and are known by those of those traditions. It is said that in Usui's group, the "Usui Reiki Ryoho Gakkai", that the symbols are known but not used. There would therefore appear to be many different practices and opinions regarding the symbols, and different lineages of Reiki seem to have evolved their own ideas regarding this.[5]

Since they can be found in abundance on any web search and have appeared in numerous books and magazines, and because I have never been asked by any of my Reiki Masters to keep them secret, I do not feel compelled to keep them as such and so I present them here for further discussion. Treating the symbols

---

[5] *Reiki II Manual.* © 1998-2001 Vincent Amador

with deep respect is a core practice in Reiki and one I hope to pass on to my students. However you decide to practice Reiki is up to you. For those who feel differently than I do I simply ask that you please afford me the basic respect to allow me to follow my own path. May the practices and principles of Reiki allow each of us to follow our own heart wherever it may take us.

THE THREE SACRED SYMBOLS OF REIKI II

Originally referred to as simply "Symbol 1", "Symbol 2", and "Symbol 3", their associated *jumon* (Japanese for "mystical incantation" or "magic spell") eventually became conflated with the symbols, and now in the West are generally considered to be their names.

The three symbols, when taken together, form a sort of map detailing the spiritual progression of the soul. They each represent specific energies present in universal life-force, but by approaching them individually we are able to focus on particular states of being.

It is now sometimes reported that Usui did not originally use the symbols, but began doing so when he was teaching students in the last years of his life, such as Chujiro Hayashi[6]. Much emphasis has been placed on the importance of the symbols in the West, even to the degree of them becoming almost deified in some eyes.

What follows are descriptions and images of the Three Sacred Symbols of Reiki II. Included are key phrases based on their function, and two alias names (Japanese and Western, respectively) that can be used in place of their "names".

---

[6] Who, of course, taught and initiated Hawayo Takata from whom all Western Reiki lineages derive.

CHO KU REI
"Place the power of the universe here"
Alias: FOCUS or POWER
Function: Gathering/increasing/directing power

The first symbol passed in Reiki is the Cho Ku Rei, (pronounced "cho koo ray") the "Power Symbol". Its exact origins are obscure; the *kanji* characters that would record its meaning are lost to antiquity and only the *jumon* remains (which records *sound* but not meaning). Depending on the particular *kanji* used, "Chokurei" has been found in Tendai Buddhism as well as in Shinto where it is associated with the power of spirits (*kami*)[7]. In Shinto the *kami* often appear as serpents which may be the origin of the theory that this symbol is styled after a coiled snake rearing its head.

---

[7] *The Reiki Symbols*, ©2002-2005 James Deacon.
http://www.aetw.org/reiki_symbolsP.html

"Chokurei" also appears as "an Empirical edict or command" indicating (spiritual) authority. Takata translated it as "put the [spiritual] power here". This symbol invokes the presence of earthly *ki* which empowers the three parts of the spiritual practitioner, (body, mind, and spirit) promoting life, power, and healing.

In regards to internal practice it gathers *ki* and directs it into the center of the healer to be stored. When directed externally, it acts as a command to focus the energy wherever the symbol is placed. It is also used to increase the flow of energy, either at the beginning of a session or at any point when the energy is perceived to be waning.

In the West it is most often referred to as "the power symbol", but if that is all that we know it as then it is all too easy to overlook the specific energy that this particular key unlocks. In Japan its alias is *Focus*; for that is exactly what this symbol does: it focuses energy and fixes it into a particular location. It helps to focus the mind; used at the beginning of a Reiki session it helps us to connect to Reiki more directly, and bring us into the right type of consciousness for channeling divine presence. Used at the end of a session it helps to pull scattered personal energies back together, helping to ground and integrate the experience.

Because of its ability to focus and direct power, this symbol is also called upon in order to remove energetic blocks, to "get everything flowing". In modern practice it is used to clear "negative" energy from people, objects, rooms, etc. as well as to further empower other symbols.

SEI HEI KI
"God and man become one"
Alias: HARMONY or MENTAL/EMOTIONAL
Function: Mental/emotional healing

The second symbol passed is Sei Hei Ki, (pronounced "say hay key") the "Harmony Symbol". Its likely origin is the Sanskrit *hrih*[8], used as a meditative focus for invoking great compassion. The *hrih* is associated with the Boddhisattva Avalokitesvara who is known as a goddess in different cultures under various names: Tara in Tibet, Kannon in Japan, and Kuan Yin in

---

[8] See James Deacon's Reiki Pages. ©2003-2004
http://www.aetw.org/reiki_symbolsME.html

China[9]. In Reiki it is used in order to promote healing to the mind and emotions, relieving stress and trauma, and even for improving memory.

This symbol invokes earthly and heavenly *ki* bringing them into harmony. This function is the origin of the often stated translation for this symbol: "God and man are united as One."

In practice, Sei Hei Ki acts as a connection between the subconscious of the Reiki practitioner and the recipient, offering healing through compassion. Even for ailments that might be considered purely physical (such as injuries or certain types of disease) there is most often an emotional root that can be most effectively addressed with the energies unlocked with this symbol. This is the symbol of pure love, used to unravel the emotional tangles of habits, patterns, and pre-conditioning. This symbol is used to assist in soothing emotional trauma as well as used to help restore higher brain function including improving memory and reasoning.

One interpretation[10] of this symbol is that it helps to balance the left and right hemispheres of the brain; the angles on the left representing the analytical left hemisphere, while the curved lines on the right represent the non-linear right hemisphere. Whether or not this was explicitly thought of when the symbol was first employed by Usui, this explanation fits with the overall meaning and use of this sacred symbol.

---

[9] *"The Sacred Usui Reiki Symbols"*, ©2009 C.J. Chow.
http://www.brigidsflame.com/reikisymbols.html
[10] *The Reiki Symbols* by Kathie Lipinski, RN.
http://www.reiki.org/reikinews/Symbols.html

HON SHA ZE SHO NEN
"The Buddha in me contacts the Buddha in you"
Alias: CONNECTION or DISTANCE
Function: Remotely linking practitioner and recipient

The third and final symbol passed in Reiki II is Hon Sha Ze Sho Nen, (pronounced "hone shah zay sho nen") the "Connection Symbol". In practice it is used to create an energetic connection between practitioner and recipient without regard to distance. In effect the meaning of this symbol identifies separation as *an illusion* and so by affirming a universal oneness a connection is made by which to send Reiki over long distances.

This symbol isn't really a symbol at all; it is a slightly condensed form of *kanji* that forms a sentence in the Japanese language. While the *essence* of its definition has sometimes been given as "No past, no present, no future" or "the Buddha in me contacts the Buddha in you", a more accurate translation is, "Correct Thought (Correct Mindfulness) is the essence of being"[11]. This expresses the premise that consciousness is the foundation of all reality.

Distant or absentee healing is one of the more exciting aspects of Reiki practice and its applications are seemingly endless. But the distances that Reiki is able to traverse are not confined to the spatial realm. The universal life-force is omnipresent and is that stuff from which space-time itself is comprised. It is a common practice to send Reiki into the past or the future as well as in the present moment, for the core of universal oneness is not simply that all space is one space, but also that all time is one time; a singular eternal moment in which exists the entirety of universal consciousness.

Before it begins to seem as if I am making claims that Reiki can change history like some sort of spiritual time machine, consider that we might send Reiki into a past situation in order to connect to and heal the hurt held in the present. By tapping into pain, anger, fear or other "negative" emotions trapped by past trauma, we can work to release them in the present. Likewise we can send Reiki into the future to assist us or others in situations that we know are likely to be stressful, such as an upcoming medical appointment, counseling session, or work meeting.

Since the root of the translation of the *jumon* is one of "right consciousness" this is also the "mental" symbol. Whereas Sei

---

[11] *The Reiki Symbols*. ©2003-2004 James Deacon.
http://www.aetw.org/reiki_symbolsD.html

Hei Ki was about harmonizing both the mental and emotional, Hon Sha Ze Sho Nen is a window into higher consciousness and may be associated by some with the Higher Self or "Buddha nature". This perspective unlocks even more possibilities of using this sacred symbol, such as to help two or more people "get along" or "see eye to eye"; utilizing its nature of connecting the Higher Selves of people or groups for healing that cannot be done on the personality level. This, along with the function of distant connection, leads me to the feeling that the key phrase given in the beginning of this section is an accurate depiction of the energy this symbol represents.

The Anatomy of the Soul

One of the ways in which we can approach the symbols is as a map detailing the anatomy of the soul. Beginning with Cho Ku Rei, we experience earthly *ki*, that which keeps our bodies alive and functioning. This is also the raw power that fuels all three parts of ourselves; as it rises to a higher vibration it becomes Sei Hei Ki, our mental and emotional selves. When these parts of ourselves are in harmony only then can we ascend into higher consciousness (Hon Sha Ze Sho Nen). Taken together the symbols are a reminder that all of our parts must be treated as holy in order to achieve the spiritual development that we seek.

How to Draw the Symbols

Much emphasis has been placed on the correct way to draw the symbols. This is largely because in the Japanese written language, the order of the strokes is an important art to master, since the calligraphy can easily become distorted if the brush lingers in between parts of the characters, essentially giving a different meaning than what was intended. In the West this is less of a concern, but still the order of the strokes is an important art to master if nothing else than simply to enhance one's discipline. In itself it is a meditation; each stroke an opportunity to bring our consciousness into a deeper resonance with the energies that each symbol unlocks.

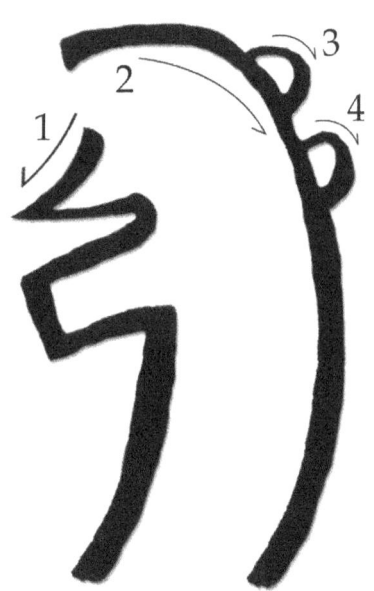

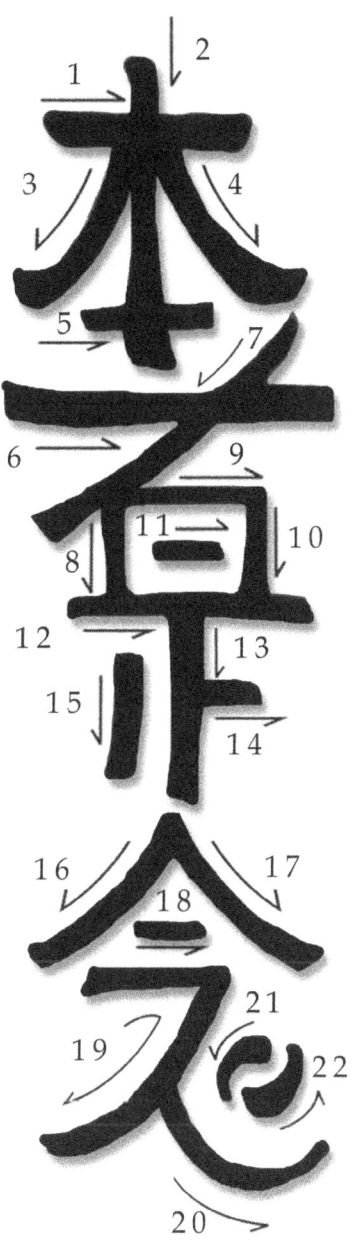

The following are exercises to strengthen your relationship with each of the symbols passed at Reiki II. **For maximum benefit they should be performed at least once a day for 30 days following your Reiki II attunement, or any time you wish to deepen your relationship with these sacred symbols.** If you have *not* yet received the Reiki II attunement you will still get some benefit from performing the exercises, but it will not be the same as for those who have received the symbols energetically during an attunement.

Drawing the Symbols #1: Memorizing the Strokes

Items needed:
- A visual guide of the symbol to be memorized that shows the correct stroke order
- A pen or pencil
- Some paper

Step 1: Begin by looking at the symbol to be memorized. In your mind's eye, imagine the process of drawing the symbol; talking care to mentally form each stroke as if you were painting them upon a canvas. Do this eight times.

Step 2: Physically draw the symbol on your paper while using the visual guide. Take your time with this! Do this eight times.

Step 3: Put your visual guide away and get a new sheet of paper. Draw the symbol from memory once and then compare it to the visual guide. If you have done it correctly then repeat this process seven more times. If you have made any errors go back to Step 2.

Drawing the Symbols #2: Auric Movements

Once we have mastered the stroke order and have committed each symbol to memory, we can add in the important step of feeling the energy. This can be done in various ways, but one of the easiest is to simply visualize them with the added step of empowering them with Reiki.

Step 1: Begin by connecting to Reiki in whatever fashion you feel most comfortable with. Gassho breathing and the Microcosmic Orbit are two methods that many Reiki practitioners employ. The Waterfall Meditation (as described in my Reiki I book) is also a good way to achieve this.

Step 2: As in the previous exercise, begin imagining the process of drawing the symbol, only this time you are sending Reiki into each stroke. For those who are visual in nature you may "see" the symbol glowing with a vibrant light. Those who process energies in a more embodied way may feel tingling or some may even "hear" the symbol. Be open to however energy manifests for you. *For example:* Cho Ku Rei may begin with an energy presence about arms-length to your left and above your head. Imagine that you can feel the flow of Reiki moving from this point as it "swoops" over to above the middle of your forehead, and then again as it "swoops" straight downward, perhaps as far as your feet before beginning the inward spiral. Notice how each stroke feels as you imagine your aura itself drawing this symbol with your energetic essence.

Step 3: Mentally or out-loud say the *jumon* three times feeling how the symbol is now activated or awakened.

Step 4: Take three deep breaths and imagine "absorbing" the symbol fully into your aura where it enhances your energy-field.

DRAWING THE SYMBOLS #3:
FEELING THE POWER THROUGH SOUND

A powerful way to activate and even increase the power that the symbols unlock is to incorporate their *jumon*. Spiritual practitioners from many different cultures incorporate the power of sound vibration into their work through the use of chanting and singing. Reiki is no different.

Step 1: Begin by connecting to Reiki.

Step 2: As above mentally draw the symbol in your aura while sending Reiki into it, only now combine the act of chanting the *jumon* of the symbol. The *jumon* should be "vibrated", that is to say that it is performed in a long, slow, low-drone so that you can feel it vibrate in your body as you vocalize. "See" the symbol shining brighter as you chant, feeling it as becoming "awakened".

Step 3: Take three deep breaths and imagine "absorbing" the symbol fully into your aura where it enhances your energy-field.

DRAWING THE SYMBOLS #4:
GESTURE AND HAND DRAWING

The most common method of utilizing the symbols is in the form of ritual gesticulation, or drawing them with the hands or fingers. This can be done for yourself in order to "activate" the symbol, or as part of a Reiki session in which a certain symbol is to be used on the client and so is drawn over the area of the body that requires the energy it represents.

Step 1: Connect to Reiki.

Step 2: Hold your dominant hand palm out away from you and feel Reiki flowing through the energy-center in the palm. Be aware that the energy flows naturally and comes to a "point" about 2-3" in front of your palm. Using this energetic point, draw your chosen symbol in the air before you while you imagine the symbol glowing with light as it hovers there. Feel it being charged with Reiki with each stroke. Feel how the energy of the symbol before you flows into your heart and up through your crown and into infinity.

Alternative: Feeling Reiki flowing through your hands and into each finger, draw your chosen symbol in the air before you while you imagine the symbol glowing with light as it hovers there. Feel it being charged with Reiki with each stroke. Feel the energy of the symbol flowing through you and up into infinity.

Step 3: Mentally intone the *jumon* three times to "activate" the symbol while you "send" it into the desired location. (This can be done by "tapping" the symbol three times, "pushing" or "nudging" the symbol with your hands or fingers, or by simply visualizing it flowing into its intended destination where it melts or is absorbed.) Your third and final intonation should occur the moment that the symbol finds its final location. Continue to send Reiki as you would normally.

OTHER METHODS OF ACTIVATING THE SYMBOLS

In addition to the above methods there are numerous other ways in which the symbols can be utilized both in sessions with clients as well as for personal development. Using the same basic techniques given here, you may find benefit in using the symbols in the following ways:

- Charge your breath with Reiki by drawing the Cho Ku Rei with your aura for three exhales, breathing them in, and then performing the Violet Breath, and exhaling a

supercharged Focus symbol. Try this with all three symbols.
- With the index finger of your dominant hand, draw the symbol(s) on the open palm of the other.
- Visualize the symbol and (mentally or out-loud) intone its name or alias three times.
- Draw the symbol with your Third Eye.
- Draw them on the roof of your mouth with your tongue. (Combined with the Violet Breath this is a powerful technique for supercharging symbols, breathing them outward and into place.)
- Say the symbol's name or alias three times.

USING THE SYMBOLS

Now that the symbols have been activated, and our relationship to them deepened, we can put them into action in our practical work.

During a session there will be times in which your intuition guides you to use a particular symbol. Perhaps you feel that the energy is slow or faint; the Focus/Power Symbol can be utilized in order to get it flowing. Or imagine that a client is suffering from grief or depression; the Harmony Symbol can be used to soothe debilitating emotional states giving emotional healing. *How* they are used is nearly unimportant; what *is* important is that you remain in the present moment and aware of how the energy is guiding you.

Some practitioners insist that each symbol used must be followed by a Focus/Power symbol in order to "activate" it. This, I believe, stems from the idea that the symbols themselves carry the power and so Harmony and Connection would require Focus in order to empower them. Since the symbols are *triggers* for aspects of Universal Life-force and not the force themselves, using a Focus/Power symbol each time is unnecessary, but again I ask you to defer to your own intuition as it arises in the moment.

Symbols may be drawn/activated/awakened any time you wish to connect to them using any of the previously mentioned methods or by some other method that you feel comfortable with.

In addition to a session they may be used in a variety of ways, some of which include:

Clearing a Crystal or Object (Jakikiri Joka ho)

Reiki can be used to energetically cleanse crystals or other objects prior to spiritual use. This is a slight variation of a traditional technique. *Please note that it is only recommended for use with non-living objects as the energies involved are traditionally deemed to be too severe and may cause discomfort if used on a living being.*

Step 1: Connect to Reiki imagining the power flowing into your *tanden* and eventually filling your whole body.

Step 2: If possible, hold the object in your non-dominant hand (if not hold your non-dominant hand palm outward facing the object) and then use (trace, visualize, intone, etc.) the Focus Symbol over it feeling it "set" into place.

Step 3: Feeling Reiki flowing through your hands, take your dominant hand and hold it horizontal in front of you with your palm facing down. Make three "karate chops" over the object in quick succession; each time ending the movement abruptly.

Step 4: Channel Reiki into the object and finish by tracing the Focus/Power Symbol over it once more.

Clearing Blocks from a Living Being

While the above exercise is great for non-living objects, sometimes blocks need to be cleared from a person's body, or even from plants or animals. In these cases you can use the following gentle technique.

Step 1: Connect to Reiki. When the block has been located perform Reiki over the area for as long as your intuition suggests.

Step 2: Trace the Focus/Power Symbol over it and then resume the Reiki flow over the area. Sending Reiki for a few to several moments is most often enough to clear all extraneous energies away, but can be performed longer if need be. The blocked area will generally feel like it softly "brightens up" when it is clear. With a little practice you will be able to sense this on your own.

Step 3: Again trace the Focus/Power Symbol over the previously blocked area and resume performing Reiki as normal.

Clearing a Space

Much like burning sage or "smudging", Reiki can be used to clear "negative" energy from your home or environment.

Step 1: Connect to Reiki. Send a Focus/Power Symbol into each of the four directions (North, East, South, and West), imagining the influence of the symbol filling that quarter before you move along to the next direction. Do this also for above and below, feeling that you have created a hollow "Reiki Bubble" in your space.

Step 2: Finish by sending a seventh Focus Symbol into the center, feeling how it fills the "bubble" and all within is cleared and blessed by Reiki.

CREATING A HEALING SPACE
Much as above except when you reach the center, use all three of the symbols and allow their energies to permeate the whole area. *This is an especially potent practice to engage in prior to performing a Reiki session, as it facilitates deeper healing and relaxation in the space.*

EMPOWERING A HEALING BATH
Reiki can transform an ordinary bath into a healing event! Performing Reiki on bath water prior to a soak is a great way to help soothe tired muscles and perhaps even help to stave off colds or flu. First, consider your environment; dim the lights, light some candles, put on some soft music. Draw a bath and then clear the water by using the Focus Symbol, sending Reiki into the water with your hands just above the surface. Next use the Harmony Symbol and "see" it glowing in the water. Send Reiki into the water until you feel it is complete. As you soak, perform the Waterfall Meditation or otherwise maintain the flow of Reiki within you.

EMPOWERING FOOD & DRINK
Using Reiki on food or beverages is an excellent way to engage in a spiritual relationship with the sustenance we put in our bodies. Using the Focus Symbol, channel Reiki into your food or drink until you feel a resonant connection. Use the Harmony Symbol and open yourself to gratitude for the food you are about to eat. Enjoy!

•

These are just some ideas for you can apply Reiki to your life. The possibilities are actually endless.

CHAPTER FOUR:
Mental & Emotional Healing

Reiki can be used for far more than simply for physical healing. Any bad habit, negative behavior, emotional pain, hurt, scar, or complex can be transformed by using the practices and power of Reiki. Sei Hei Ki, the Harmony or Mental/Emotional Symbol is specifically keyed into the vibration that can heal issues in our emotional reality. This symbol and the energies that it represents can be utilized in a myriad of ways. What follows is an exercise to deepen your relationship with this symbol, as well as prepare you for performing healing on mental and/or emotional issues.

EMOTIONAL HEALING
Step 1: Connect to Reiki.

Step 2: Recall whatever emotional issue you wish to work on. If performing this for a client, instruct them to recall whatever issue they feel is causing them trouble, or at the very least the feelings that are produced by the issue. Imagine the light of Reiki infusing the situation and feelings with healing light.

Step 3: Activate the Focus/Power Symbol and feel its power in your palms and above your crown. Do the same with the Connection Symbol.

Step 4: Activate the Harmony (Mental/Emotional) Symbol and feel Reiki flowing into the situation or "negative" feelings. Feel the symbol radiating and sending Universal Love and Compassion into the feelings and situation.

Step 5: Use Sei Hei Ki at several (if not all) positions on the body that you feel compelled to treat (or at every hand position if you are using set hand positions). Feel its healing power flowing into the negative emotions, thoughts, and situations. Do this for as long as you feel is necessary.

Step 6: Finish by using the Focus Symbol over the client's midsection in order to "ground and center" their energies.

MENTAL HEALING

Though Sei Hei Ki is most often referred to in the West as the "Mental/Emotional Healing Symbol", Hon Sha Ze Sho Nen also plays an important role in mental healing as well. While we will focus on its uses for distant or absentee healing in the next chapter, the Connection Symbol calls forth the presence of higher consciousness, assisting us in "raising our conscious vibrations", thus helping us rise above mental blocks that keep us trapped in out-dated patterns and conditioning. Using this symbol we can more easily send messages to our Higher Selves so that all aspects of our consciousness can participate in our development and healing.

Step 1: Connect to Reiki. Activate the Connection Symbol and see it shining above your head as a connective power between your personality and your Higher Self.

Step 2: Recall whatever mental issue you wish to heal. Beam Reiki from the Connection Symbol above you and into this area of your life. If working on a client imagine this light likewise permeating their life to heal issues that stem from the past. You may also wish to activate the Harmony Symbol.

Step 3: Perform Reiki normally.

Step 4: Finish by using the Focus Symbol to bring all energies back, "grounding and centering" them.

THOUGHT EMPOWERMENT #2 (*SEIHEIKI CHIRYO HO*)

This is essentially the same exercise as the Thought Empowerment #1 (Nentatsu ho) exercise learned in Level One, but with the added benefit of the symbols. Try alternating between the two exercises and feel for yourself whatever differences or similarities you experience. As always, this can be done for a client or for yourself, if desired.

Step 1: Identify some area of your life that is giving you or your client trouble. It can be anything, big or small. Some examples include bad habits, negative thought patterns ("I'm too weak!" "I'm not good enough!" "I always have bad luck!") or even relationships that are hurtful or undermine our sense of self-worth. Take some time to really reflect on this negative condition.

Step 2: Create a *positive* affirmation designed to take precedence over the "negative" condition. (For example: If dealing with fear one might use: "I am courageous". If depression is an issue you might affirm: "I live in joy", etc.)

Step 3: Connect to Reiki and bow in reverence to your client.

Step 4: With your dominant hand draw the Focus/Power Symbol over the client's occipital ridge (where the skull meets the spine). Place your hand over this area and let Reiki flow.

Step 5: When you intuitively feel it is time to move forward, remove your hand and draw the Harmony Symbol in the same area and then another Focus/Power Symbol. Replace your hand, letting Reiki flow through that symbol and into the client's brain.

Step 6: Mentally repeat the positive affirmation while you place your non-dominant hand on the client's forehead at their hairline, letting Reiki flow from each hand to balance and empower the affirmation.

Step 7: Continue for as long as your intuition dictates. Finish by again bowing in reverence.

•

Beyond the exercises given here feel free to experiment with the healing power of these symbols. By working with them in different ways our own spiritual path unfolds before us, taking us into new vistas of thought and possibility.

CHAPTER FIVE:
Distant Healing

One of the most exciting aspects of the Reiki tradition is the ability to send it over long distances.

The Connection or Distant Symbol is used in Western Reiki practice to create an etheric connection between the practitioner and a recipient through which energy may be sent.

When performing Reiki at a distance, there are some things to consider; the more information that you have about the intended the better, such as their name, location, etc. Whatever you can obtain that you feel would be a symbolic link can become an actual link when empowered with energy.

There are two basic methods for distance Reiki, and a third that is a combination of the first two. Whatever method you choose to employ, a good way to begin a session, of course, is to first connect to Reiki. When you feel sufficiently charged, awaken the Connection Symbol by drawing it in the air, visualization, chanting, etc. and feel it connecting you to the intended recipient, recalling their name, face, mannerisms, location, "vibe", etc. –whatever you can recall about them that can provide a mental link.

REIKI BY PROXY

A proxy is a substitute for the actual thing, and when performing Reiki by proxy this means that we are using a symbolic substitute as a "stand in" for the person in question. Reiki is performed just as you would if the person was physically present, with the exception that an object is used; a doll, a photograph... or another personal link such as an article of clothing, a sample of their handwriting, a lock of hair –anything that they have owned or touched that contains some amount of life-force.

Step 1: Clear the energies in the proxy by using the Focus Symbol.

Step 2: Next, identify the proxy with the person by surrounding it with energy and using the Connection Symbol. "See" (and/or feel) their essence flowing into the proxy and becoming "one" with it. When you feel it has "sunken in" use the Focus Symbol again with the idea of focusing the energies and grounding them into the proxy, "sealing" it.

Step 3: Perform Reiki as you normally would if the person were with you. When finished, send the essence of the person back to them with the Connection Symbol and then clear the proxy with Focus.

ASTRAL REIKI

For those who are inclined to work with astral travel[12] you may be interested in utilizing this other method of distant healing.

As in the above example we will again be working with the energetic essence of an intended recipient who is not physically present, only this time we will be travelling to them, as opposed to summoning their energetic presence to us.

Step 1: Connect to Reiki.

Step 2: Activate the Connection Symbol. "See" it flowing to your *tanden* (located beneath your navel) where your life-force gathers. Activate it again and send it to your heart, and again to a space above your head. Feel all three as different reflections of the same energy which is your spiritual essence.

---

[12] For more information about astral travel please read *Soul Flight* by Donald Tyson and *Mastering Astral Projection* by Robert Bruce and Brian Mercer.

Step 3: Allow yourself to travel astrally to the desired location where you will perform Reiki on the intended recipient in whatever fashion you normally would.

Step 4: When finished, activate the Connection Symbol once more and feel yourself travelling back into your own physical body.

Step 5: Use the Focus symbol on yourself to ensure that your energy field is cleared, charged, and whole.

REIKI ASTRAL PROXY MORPH[13]

This technique is really just a blend of the other two given here but there are two basic ways to accomplish this. The first uses astral space instead of a physical proxy; we imagine the person in front of us and then perform Reiki with all of the physical movements we would normally use. To an outsider this will appear as if we are waving our hands about in the air.

The second version of this technique is to simply utilize the energies in trance, visualizing the person in front of you as you perform Reiki in the trance state. In this you may wish to imagine a "healing temple" or other soothing and spiritual location in which to perform the session so as to "boost" the energies involved. When re-visited, this internal place of power can become quite potent and will carry a healing vibration of its own that can assist you in your work.

REIKI LISTS

This is a modern technique by which we can easily send Reiki to several people or places at once. Simply write down as much information as you can about a person and their situation; name, age, location, issue, etc. If you have a photograph so much the

---

[13] Much thanks to Reiki Master Carrie Hammond for giving voice to this idea in her book *Blue Fire Reiki: The Reiki II Handbook*. ©2006 Carrie Hammond.

better. Do this for any other people or situations that you wish and place these lists together in some special place such as an altar, shelf, or box dedicated to this work. Every day activate the Connection Symbol over the lists to forge a link and then use the Focus/Power Symbol, and then Harmony. Send Reiki for as long as you'd like. Finish by using the Focus/Power Symbol once more.

BEAMING

This is a technique by which we send Reiki from our hands at a distance but with the recipient in the room with us. This can be done across the room as long as they are in our line of sight, or immediately over the person (such as when working in the aura, or further away.) Simply use the Connection Symbol in each of your palms and then send Reiki through them as beams of light emanating from the energy-centers there. Perform Reiki as normal.

GROUP DISTANCE HEALING

Distance healing can be done with a group just as local healing can. Once simple method is to gather in a circle and then place some object of focus in the center that represents the recipient (as in Reiki Proxy Healing). Alternatively you may simply instruct the group to visualize the intended recipient as being in the center of the circle. Using the Connection Symbol all members activate the symbol in their palms and then use the Beaming technique in order to send Reiki into the proxy (or visual image).

REIKI THROUGH TIME

Another aspect of the Connection Symbol is its use in sending Reiki without regard to the limitations of time as well as of space.

Step 1: Connect to Reiki. Breathe it down into your *tanden* and allow it to radiate throughout your entire body and aura.

Step 2: Activate the Connection Symbol and visualize where you wish to send Reiki. If, for example, your intent is to send it into the past at the moment of an accident or other stressful event, make that intent clear in your mind or speak it out loud. Do the same for sending to future times. If possible, visualize the location. (Remember, you can also send Reiki to yourself in the past or future!)

Step 3: With your connection established, perform Reiki as you would for a distant treatment, using whatever symbols you feel are appropriate.

Step 4: When finished use the Focus/Power Symbol to "gather up" any extraneous energies.

•

Many other methods for distance healing exist. Use your imagination and remember to let your intuition guide you.

CHAPTER SIX:
Additional Techniques, Part 2

While previously we have worked primarily by directing Reiki with our hands, Mikao Usui taught that Reiki could emanate from any part of the body, but most strongly from the hands, eyes, and breath.

THE REIKI BREATH (KOKI HO)

There are times when physical touch would be inappropriate for use in a session with a client. Perhaps in the case of burns or open wounds this might be so but especially in the case of certain types of abuse when even the close proximity of the practitioner's hands may trigger negative results. In these cases we can effectively use the Reiki Breath method.

Step 1: Connect to Reiki. Feel it fill your whole body with light.

Step 2: Bring your attention to the area that requires treatment and generate heart-felt compassion for your client.

Step 3: Breathe in gently through the nose all the way down to your *tanden*, gathering Reiki in that area.

Step 4: Purse your lips and exhale gently, blowing out not only your breath but the light of Reiki as well. Direct this breath to the intended area, feeling that compassion bathing the client like a healing salve.

Addition: You may wish to utilize symbols along with this technique by tracing them on the roof of your mouth with your tongue where you visualize them glowing brightly and then gently blowing them out into the intended area(s) where they set into place or otherwise are absorbed.

Reiki Gazing (Gyoshi Ho)

Reiki Gazing, or "Gyoshi ho" (literally "Method of Staring"; usually translated as "Method of Healing with the Eyes") is a simple and powerful technique that can be employed any time physical touch is not possible or desired. This is an original technique taught by Usui.

Many varied energies can be transmitted via the eyes. Consider those times when you may have experienced an odd sensation only to find that someone has been staring at you. While not the same energy that we are utilizing in Reiki, this should give an idea of the possibility of energy being transmitted from the eyes via the line of sight.

Step 1: Open to Reiki. With softly defocused eyes, gaze at the area you wish to send energy to.

Step 2: Feel love and compassion pouring through your eyes and going to the recipient. Imagine them perfect, in balance, and whole.

Step 3: Visualize the symbols you wish to use moving out from your eyes and flowing into in the area of your gaze.

Step 4: Continue until you are inspired to move to the next position or until you feel the session is finished.

Cultivating Spiritual Power (Hatsurei-ho)

Hatsu can be defined as, "to generate something"; *Rei* as, "spirit or soul"; *Ho* means, "method, or way." This is a technique from Usui that cleanses the energy body and generates a greater current of Reiki energy.

Step 1: *Relaxation*
Sit comfortably in a chair or on the floor. Close your eyes and relax. Place your attention onto your *tanden* (located 2 " below navel and 1" inside the body). Place your hands on your lap with your palms down.

Step 2: *Focusing the Mind*
Say to yourself something to the effect of: "I now begin the Cultivation exercise (or Hatsurei-ho)."

Step 3: *Dry bathing*
1. Place the palm of your right-hand flat on top of your left shoulder.
2. Breathe in. Hold your breath as you move your hand downward in a diagonal line, from your left shoulder across your heart-center and to your right hip. Now, forcefully release your breath, and vigorously shake your hand as you move it off of your body.
3. Repeat the above movements with your left hand, on the right side of your body.
4. Now place your right hand palm down on the middle of your left forearm, hand flat, fingertips pointing outwards.
5. Take a deep breath. Hold your breath as you move your right hand, down your arm, to the fingertips, keeping the left arm straight and parallel to the floor in front of you. Again, forcefully release your breath and shake your hand vigorously as you move off the body.
6. Repeat the above movements with your left hand on your right arm.
7. Repeat movements 5 and 6 again.

Step 4: Connect to Reiki (*Bringing in the Light*)
With your hands raised above your head, visualize and feel the light of Reiki flowing down from the heavens, through your

hands and into your whole body, moving through you as a river of light.

Step 5: *Cleansing Breath*
1. With your relaxed hands palms up on your lap, breathe through your nose while focusing on your *tanden*. Relax with every breath.
2. While breathing in, imagine the light of Reiki as it enters your crown, moves to your *tanden* and expands until your entire body is filled with Reiki light, completely dissolving all tensions, worry, and concern.
3. On your exhale, imagine the light of Reiki expanding beyond your skin, filling your aura and then radiating outward in all directions into infinity.
4. Repeat as many times as you would like.

Step 6: Gassho - *Prayer mudra*
Put your hands palms together in the prayer position in front of and slightly above your heart-center.

Step 7: *Concentration Breath*
For this step the hands remain in the Gassho position; imagine that you are breathing *through* your hands.

1. While breathing in, visualize the Light of Reiki (or white light) entering your hands and flowing down to the *tanden*, expanding until *tanden* is filled with Reiki Light.
2. On your exhale, visualize light moving from the *tanden* to the hands filling them with Reiki Light, and flowing outwards in all directions.
3. Repeat for a couple of minutes or as long as you like.

Step 8: *Focusing the Mind*
Place hands back on lap palms down. Say to yourself something to the effect of: "I have finished the cultivation exercise (Hatsurei-ho)."

Reiki Detox (Tanden Chiryo Ho)

When working with Reiki or any other form of "energy medicine" detoxification does not only refer to the purging of tangible physical substances from one's being, but emotional, psychological, and spiritual 'toxins' as well.

This technique not only starts the detoxification process but also revitalizes the client's *tanden*.

Step 1: Rest your hands, palms down, on your thighs. Close your eyes and focus your attention on your *tanden*. Relax and softly focus on your breath.

Step 2: Connect to Reiki and feel the energy flowing through your entire being.

Step 3: Bow in reverence and make a silent statement of intention that you begin this treatment for the healing and well-being of the client.

Step 4: Standing on the client's left, place your left hand on the area of their *tanden*, and your right hand on their forehead. Be aware of Reiki flowing through your hands.

Step 5: Silently affirm that all toxins, blockages, and impurities be *gently* cleared from the client.

Step 6: Keeping your hands in this position, continue to be aware of the flow of Reiki until you sense a balancing of the energy between your hands. This may take only a moment, or it may take several minutes. When you can feel the same level of intensity from each of your hands, gently remove your right hand from the client's forehead and place it on top of your left hand on their *tanden*. Continue for as long as you intuit it is appropriate, generally anywhere from 5-20 minutes.

Step 7: To conclude, bow in reverence silently affirming gratitude for the opportunity to help your client heal themselves.

Combing

It is likely that in your Level One practice you have already discovered this simple technique. Quite literally, Combing is the act of loosely running your fingers through a person's aura so as to "fluff" or "detangle" the energetic fibers of the auric field so as to cause the personal energy of the recipient to move smoothly. With Reiki flowing through your hands simply drag your loose fingers through their aura from the crown to the feet, repeating the process several times. This is a great way to end a session as it leaves the recipient feeling aligned and refreshed.

•

At this point you will have accumulated a wealth of knowledge concerning the practices of Reiki. But Reiki is so much more than knowledge. Like any true spiritual path Reiki affords us an opportunity to move beyond knowledge and into the blooming lotus of wisdom. If we have been applying the practices and Principles to our work and daily lives then we will have begun to move beyond the outer form of specific practices and into the realm of *reiji*, of 'guidance of spirit'. In this Reiki itself moves beyond Reiki the tradition and into something more, that shining light of divine presence that must manifest uniquely for each of us.

CHAPTER SEVEN:
Ethics

Ethics is an important subject to consider when dealing with any spiritual system, especially one that is geared toward personal development and healing. In my Reiki I manual I discuss the importance of using accurate terms and titles to describe oneself (Example: I call myself a "Reiki Practitioner" and NOT a "Reiki Healer"). If we truly understand that it is not us that are doing the "healing" then we honestly have no right calling ourselves healers. (For those of you who may be healers in other systems this obviously does not apply to you.) As of the time of this writing, Reiki is the only formal healing technique that I perform and since I know that I am simply a channel for Reiki, and that it is Reiki that is providing an opportunity for the client to *heal themselves*, then to call myself a "healer" is misleading at best, and fraudulent at worst. Some practitioners might have nothing but the best intentions going in but consider that there may be a situation in which a client comes to you for a session out of desperation; long-term or even terminal illness can drive otherwise balanced and level-headed individuals into behavior that is somewhat questionable and should this happen and the practitioner is referring to themselves as a "healer" there is at the very least potential for confusion and perhaps even unrealistic expectations that can lead in some cases to false hope. It is in these extreme cases that the most damage can be done, both to the client's well-being, and to the practitioner reputation and even legal standing. Do yourself and your clients a favor and be mindful about the words that you choose to describe yourself and what you do.

ASKING PERMISSION?
Though I previously dealt with this issue in my Reiki I manual, now that the possibility of distant sessions presents itself here at the second level, I feel compelled to revisit the discussion.

From my book, *Awakening the BlueLotus:*

> One question that often comes up in discussion with Reiki practitioners is whether or not it is ethical to give Reiki before asking permission. In my training in various spiritual traditions I have often heard that it is necessary to ask someone's permission before sending them healing, blessings, etc. To do otherwise, some say, is interfering with the free-will of the recipient. In this mode of thinking, it would be necessary to ask permission before sending Reiki to an individual lest you interfere with their free-will.

There are many opinions on all sides of this issue and often times heated emotions can arise from these opinions. I can honestly say that I myself have been on both sides of this issue at one time or another. This, I think, puts me in a special position of being able to see more clearly the various points of view involved.

In my experience with different spiritual systems, the idea of free-will is often invoked as that which should never be circumvented under any circumstances. We are often told that to do so is akin to black magic, a charge that is usually accompanied by threats of karmic or spiritual retribution.

Let us assume for a moment that it's possible for one to circumvent someone's free-will using spiritual energies. Certainly in paths such as sorcery and witchcraft this possibility exists, at least on the surface; prayers and spells are often directed by one's personal intent which could have an effect on the target with or without their permission. But Reiki is somewhat different. We are not in charge of how Reiki manifests itself, at least not on the level of the personality. The practices and principles of Reiki ensure that the universal life-force is directed *by a higher spiritual power* and this power is concerned with the good of all. Circumventing someone's free-will is really not an option.

While I have formed my opinions based on personal observation using the tools from many different spiritual teachings, this is admittedly a belief that I hold and as such is subject to my personal biases. I do not put this forward as a type of dogma, but more as an explanation of where I am coming from. All any of us can do is to act from where we are. If we have worked to cleanse ourselves of "negative" conditioning then we are in a better position to respond mindfully in any given situation instead of from a place of fear, ego, and control.

Again, from my previous book:

> It is not the place of *BlueLotus*, or anyone for that matter, to dictate to anyone what they should or should not do in any particular situation. As sentient beings it is up to us to decide for ourselves what we should do. With this in mind I give you the following to consider: To decide that it is *always* necessary to ask for permission before giving Reiki is a type of blanket rule which, when evenly applied to every situation, *brings us out of the present moment*; we are then relying on a static decree that effectively traps our awareness in the past. If the practices of Reiki are geared toward being in the present moment, then it seems to me that in the present moment is where we will find our answers to whatever questions may arise in a given situation. The decision of whether or not to give Reiki, then, is situational.

I hope that his gives you something to consider regarding this issue. It is likely that at some point someone will bring up this very issue and hopefully when they do you will have already had the opportunity to release fear, worry, anger, and doubt and thus be able to make a decision for yourself based on real information of the moment, and not from the ego conditionings of the past. Whatever you decide to do, do so with the blessings Reiki has to offer.

COMPENSATION AND ENERGY EXCHANGE

Reiki II is often called "the Professional Practitioner Level" for it is at this level that many begin to perform Reiki as a business. In reality Reiki II is all that most people will need in order to perform sessions professionally.

While most practitioners of healing modalities charge for their time and expertise, the fact that Reiki is first and foremost a spiritual art can muddy the issue for some people. I have heard people claim that all spiritual sessions, classes, attunements, and instruction should be given away without monetary charge or else it is "not spiritual", citing the corrupting influence of money. I have also heard people say that if these things were given away for free then the recipients would not honor and respect them and so it is *required* that a fee be charged.

The tradition of Reiki has a history that involves money and it's not always been pretty. One argument for charging a fee is expressed in the idea of an *energy exchange* which states that if the practitioner gives a healing then there must be some sort of compensation in order to keep things in balance; I give you something then you give me something of equal value. To do anything less, we are told, will run the risk of creating imbalance in the universe.

We are also reminded of Mikao Usui's time in the "Beggar's Quarters" in which he "realized" that those whom he had healed for free did not value the healing and so returned to an unhealthy lifestyle There was no incentive for them to keep themselves healthy if they could just go and go to the free Reiki clinic and so (we are told) that Usui decided that Reiki practitioners *must* charge for their services. Later this idea was codified even further to the extent that some Reiki Masters insist that if money or another form of compensation doesn't change hands then it "isn't really Reiki"!

I'd like to address a couple of these issues head-on. First let us consider the *energy exchange* idea. First of all, *there is no such thing as an energy exchange in Reiki*. When I channel Reiki into a client *I am also receiving Reiki*, so there is no additional "exchange" necessary. In fact, with this world-view I technically *shouldn't* charge for the session because *I already received something of equal value*. In fact I already received *the exact same thing*. So the idea of an "energy exchange" as justification for charging for my Reiki services is cleanly blown out of the water.

Second, let us consider the story of the "Beggar's Quarters". First I'm going to go on record to say that I don't believe this story for an instant. Like much of the mythical history of Reiki that was put forward as "fact" in the 80's and 90's (and sadly even today in some circles) it just doesn't hold water. We were originally told that Usui worked "for seven years" in the poorest parts of the country before coming to his lucrative conclusions, but it simply does not fit the timeline that we now know to be true. While he did perform healing work for free for those who were victims of the great earthquake of 1923 we know that he later opened a clinic and taught Reiki before passing away in 1926! So there was certainly no "seven year" period involved. Remember that he founded Reiki in 1922!

This, like the assertions that Usui was a "Christian missionary" are false statements that perhaps can best be understood if we approach them as "teaching stories". But what exactly is the lesson here?

One argument that is consistently brought up in relation to the issue of charging for Reiki is that the recipient must pay a fee in order to fully appreciate that what they are receiving is of value.

If they feel it has value then they will honor it... if they don't, then they won't and will likely not alter their unhealthy behaviors in favor of healthy ones. This does sound like it is of the same flavor as the story of the "Beggar's Quarters" which is something that is common knowledge in general marketing: namely if the price tag says it is valuable then people will treat it as valuable. It is a very real psychology that can be demonstrated and replicated scientifically.

While I understand that in many cases this is true, it is quite a leap to evenly apply this to everyone in all cases, and quite another leap in order to reach the belief in the statement so often made by some "Traditional" Western Reiki practitioners that a free session "isn't Reiki".

Certainly there are those who would value Reiki who simply cannot afford sessions. If we maintain a belief system that states that only those who can pay for a session can receive the healing then we are enshrining a system that negatively impacts the poor and it is likely that they are in the most need of healing.

Being the good Pisces Sun and Gemini Moon that I am, I can see both sides of this argument. It is not my place to tell anyone what they "should" do. But since I am a teacher of this path and this is my book I will use this opportunity to once again give my insights on this often thorny issue. I think you should do what you want. Ultimately it's your choice. If you want to charge a fee, then by all means charge a fee. If you wish to give it away for free then more power to you. Whatever you decide to do just make sure that you are doing so with your eyes open and that you are doing it for the right reasons instead of hiding behind some false ideology that can be easily picked apart with little effort. There is nothing wrong with charging for your time and efforts. I certainly charge for both sessions and attunements. But I make no fancy justification involving the state of the universe when I do so; I charge because it's part of how I make my living. Until my landlord begins accepting Reiki sessions in lieu of rent then I will charge for my time, thank you very much.

With that said I also feel that as spiritual practitioners we should also "give something back"; to this end my husband and I host a monthly Reiki Share where no one is turned away for lack of funds. I also do barter and trade for hardship cases for both sessions and attunements, and truth be told I also give away sessions (and even attunements!) for free depending on the situation. In this I feel that I have struck a balance that works for me; not out of some supposed fear of universal inequality, but an internal state of harmony that allows me to deepen my work, which in reality is what Reiki is all about anyway.

CHAPTER EIGHT:
The Professional Practitioner

At Level Two you are empowered to begin a professional career as a Reiki practitioner should you choose to do so. While a career in the spiritual healing arts can be a nourishing and fulfilling one, there are many concerns that should be addressed before taking the leap into becoming a professional Reiki practitioner.

Once you have received your Level Two attunement, have fulfilled the post-attunement obligations, have received your Reiki II certificate and have mastered all of the symbols and exercises given in this manual, then you are ready to begin the process of setting up shop as a professional Reiki provider.

LEGALITIES

The first step toward setting up a Reiki business should be to research the legalities that govern your particular area. Some U.S. states require special licensing for those who offer alternative and natural health therapies. Because Reiki is a spiritual practice you may wish to consider becoming an ordained minister in order to better protect your right to practice your spiritual and religious freedom, but keep in mind that this will not automatically protect you if you are not in compliance with local laws and ordinances. The only true protection is education.

The International Center for Reiki Training (www.Reiki.org) has provided some excellent information pertaining to the practice of Reiki both for personal development as well as for those who are pursuing Reiki as a business. In particular you should read "Keeping Reiki Free" by William Rand. In this well researched article, Rand reveals some interesting and potentially troubling details concerning governmental restrictions of professional Reiki practice. You can find a PDF version of this by visiting the following web address:

www.reiki.org/Download/KeepingReikiFree.pdf

One good way to become further educated on local laws and guidelines is to contact your local chamber of commerce or city hall. Find out what laws govern the practice of spiritual energy-work. For example: some locations govern Reiki with the same laws and ordinances that govern massage while others may group Reiki practitioners with nurses or other medical providers. It is imperative that you do your homework and learn all you can about how your state, county, or city views the practices of Reiki and other alternative healing practices.

When setting up any business you will need to obtain a business license from your city, county, or state. In addition you may wish to purchase liability insurance in order to protect you from possible law suits. Even though Reiki can do no harm we have no control over what someone may do in any given situation and insurance is available to help protect us from the unforeseeable. Most massage therapists and body workers are required to have insurance in order to operate and even if you are not it is still a good idea. "An ounce of prevention is worth a pound of cure."

It is also a good idea to have new clients sign a consent form that details that Reiki is not a substitute for medical or psychological care, as well as detailing in general terms what will happen in the Reiki session. Some states require this condition and that you specifically state that you are not a licensed healing arts practitioner. Again check your local laws concerning alternative health therapies. A sample form that you may use as a generalized template is given below. Full-sized versions may be downloaded from my website at: www.faerywolf.com/misc/ReikiConsentForm.pdf

Reiki Client Consent Form

I, the undersigned, understand that Reiki is a spiritual practice used primarily as a relaxation and stress reduction technique. I acknowledge that treatments administered are only for the purpose of helping me relax and to relieve stress and while stress relief and relaxation are beneficial for the healing process I understand that Reiki treatments are NOT a substitute for medical or psychological examination, diagnosis or treatment. I am advised to seek assistance from professionals in those fields for any ailment that I may have.

I understand that Reiki practitioners are not licensed medical providers and do not diagnose conditions, nor do they prescribe substances or perform medical treatment, nor interfere with the treatment of licensed medical professionals.

I understand that Reiki is a spiritual energy methodology, which involves the laying on of hands to administer. I understand that I will be fully clothed during the session, and experience a series of "safe" hand positions (excluding the genitals and breasts) on and/or above my body that have been approved by me prior to the session.

I agree to hold as exempt the Reiki practitioner from any and all liability for any damages both real and imagined as a result, both direct and indirect, from the services rendered on or after the date stated below.

Signed: _____ Date: _____

Print Name: _____

Phone: _____ Email: _____

Notes:

_____

_____

_____

•

Location, Location, Location

You will of course need to decide where you will actually perform your sessions. Will you be working in an office or out of your home? While working from home is a dream of many practitioners it certainly comes with its own pitfalls and challenges. Will you wish to invite strangers into where you live? Do you have a separate space from your living quarters in which to perform sessions? What about residential zoning laws in your area that govern home-based businesses?

Likewise there are certain things to consider when choosing an outside office space in which to work. Is the location itself accessible? Does it have adequate parking? Will clients be able to relax and feel safe in this environment? One recommendation is to seek out a space that caters to massage therapy or other holistic health modalities as these are generally in resonance with the practices of Reiki.

Equipment and Supplies

Probably the most important piece of equipment that you will need for your Reiki practice is a massage table. How you plan to practice Reiki will determine exactly what kind you need; will you be travelling to the client's home or other location to offer your services? If so then you will need a portable table, carrying case, etc. In addition you will need sheets for your table, and perhaps other accessories such as a face rest attachment, a swivel chair, or even pillows.

A massage chair might be a good option for you as well. While generally not a substitute for a massage table, a chair can be a nice addition as it is more portable (even more so than a portable table) and is well suited for doing shorter treatments which will impact the pricing of a session, potentially widening your appeal to the general public. Massage chairs also take up less room and are ideal for situations in which you may be offering services at an event or temporary location. And since they are less expensive than a table, you may wish to purchase a massage chair first as you build up your clientele, forgoing the table until you have better established your practice.

Another thing that you should consider is water. As we learned in Level One, part of a Reiki session involves the gentle movement of toxins out of the recipient's body. One simple way to assist these toxins being flushed out of the system is to follow each session with drinking plenty of water. You may wish to provide fresh drinking water to your clients either in bottled form, or (preferably) from one of those refillable dispensers. I say that this is preferable simply because of the sheer waste that is involved in bottled water with many millions of plastic bottles ending up in landfills (and in the oceans!) across our beautiful planet. Remember that final Reiki Principle, "Be kind to all living things." Remember also that we can embody that kindness not only in the context of a session or in how we treat each other, but also in the choices that we make each day. Do the planet a favor and choose to forgo adding more plastic bottles to its already over-stressed ecosystem.

Another item that will probably be needed is tissues. I can't recall how many times I forgot this simple thing when I was beginning my Reiki practice. Since Reiki brings things up sometimes a client will experience an emotional upwelling during or immediately after the session. It's a good idea to have tissues on hand to keep them comfortable as well as to keep your environment as clean and sanitary as possible.

Other things that you may wish to include are:

- Aromatherapy oils and diffusers
    - Some practitioners prefer to set the energetic "tone" of the working space by including nice gentle scents in the room. Just be mindful that many people are scent sensitive and can have

adverse reactions to certain scents. Always consult with your client prior to using incense or oils during a session.

- Music and a sound system
  - Often Reiki practitioners will include gentle music as a means to assist the client in being able to relax. There are many titles available that have been composed specifically for Reiki sessions. A list of some of these titles appears at the end of this book.

- Candles
  - Candles are a nice touch for any space in which spiritual work is to be done. They add a sense of ambience to a room and can also assist in relaxation as candlelight is far more gentle than the harsh lighting that often accompanies an office space. Fluorescent lights, for example, can agitate the mind and interfere with the gentle work being done in a Reiki session. Just remember that some candles are scented and so might also interfere with those clients who are scent sensitive. When in doubt, use unscented candles!

- Bells, Tuning Forks, Crystals, and other spiritual tools
  - While not a part of traditional Reiki practice, many practitioners successfully employ tools from other modalities of spiritual development in their Reiki work. Bells, chimes, and tuning forks can be used to assist in balancing chakras, while crystals can be used to assist in releasing negative energies from the aura as well as implanting specific vibrations into the energy field to assist

in manifesting energies for healing and development. If you already work with tools from other spiritual paths, experiment and see how they might be of use in a Reiki session.

ADVERTISING

Once you have gathered your tools, set up your space and attended to all of the legal details that are required, you are ready to start accepting clients! But unless you already have a following you will need to let people know who you are and how to find you. Advertising is the key, and there are many ways to go about this.

The first thing that you should do is to get business cards. This is probably the single most important step that you can take for advertising your services as business cards go hand in hand with the most effective and long lasting advertising tool of which nothing else can compare: word of mouth. Your friends, family, and eventually your clients themselves will be the biggest driving force for bringing in business provided you conduct yourself in a professional manner and offer services that are worth your fees. Having business cards enables them to refer others to you and over time this will build up your clientele more reliably than any other method.

If you are artistically inclined you can opt to design your own and print them on those perforated sheets that you can find in an office supply store, or you can use an internet service and upload your design for them to print. For a more professional look you can choose a service to design them for you. I recommend and use VistaPrint.com for my business cards. They even have a "free" option in which all you pay for is shipping.

One easy (and relatively inexpensive) step that you can take for advertising your services is to get a website. Even if you are not proficient in web design you can at least have a single page that has a picture (preferably of you and your working space) a short bio, rates, and contact information. There are numerous web services available that can take this to the next level for you, beginning from free ad-driven sites, to more professional web services.

Your website should be pleasing to the eye but also have content that is of interest to your potential (and existing) clients. Articles concerning the work that you do... related artwork... even meditations and a blog... these are but a few examples of what you may wish to provide to your clients via your home on the web. Remember that your website is a virtual business card but also so much more; it is your opportunity to distinguish yourself from the rest of the world, letting your clients know who you are and what you do.

Getting your own domain name is essential for "branding" and ease of recognition. I own several domain names for the various works that I perform (Faerywolf.com, BlueLotusReiki.com, ModernConjure.com, etc.) each being easy to remember as your potential clients will need this information in order to initially find you in the chaos that is the world wide web.

Having a newsletter is also a great way to advertise as it keeps your existing clients informed about events and special offers. Having this as an email service means less overhead for you which means more of your income will be profit. Remember that content is the key; you don't want to *just* advertise your services... you will want to give something away for free as well. Again, articles, meditations, or other content of interest to your clients is a good way to keep people reading your work and thus becoming more interested in what it is that you do.

SETTING RATES & ACCEPTING PAYMENT

Since this section is about providing Reiki as a profession it would not be complete without the discussion of rates. Charging a fee for services rendered is an essential part of any business and Reiki is no different. If you feel that these services should always be free then how are you going to pay for your rent? For your equipment? For the supplies involved? If you are independently wealthy and do not need to concern yourself with such things then you may wish to provide your services free of charge. If you choose to charge for your services, then you will need to determine what you feel is a fair price for your time and efforts.

One first step is to check out the local competition. If there are other professional Reiki practitioners in your area then check out their websites and advertisements to determine what they are charging. You will want to be competitive but also charge enough to make a profit after your expenses are paid. How much is an hour session going for locally? A half hour? Are local practitioners offering discounts for bulk packages? What can you offer to make your services worth just as much as what others are offering? You may also wish to schedule appointments with other Reiki practitioners so that you can get a feel for how they are operating. Make sure that you don't undercut them; besides being rude (you wouldn't want some new upstart undercutting *your* business) you may find yourself in the position of needing to work with other local practitioners in the future and stealing someone else's clients doesn't generally lead to feelings of bliss and camaraderie.

At the time of this writing (December, 2010) my price structure is: $75 for a full session (one hour), $65 for 45 minutes, and half sessions and distant treatments are $45 (30 minutes each).

Once you determine your price structure then you will need to accept payment. Obviously cash and checks are easy, but don't rule out accepting credit cards. Though it can initially be expensive to set up, as your business booms you may wish to accept them as they are convenient and most people tend to use that as their payment choice. While you may not be able to accept them initially, on option that you may wish to look into is to use an internet-based service such as PayPal. With PayPal you can accept pre-payments for your services and your client can use their credit card to fund the transaction. Eventually you may wish to include taking credit cards directly.

CONCLUSION

Whether you decide to offer Reiki professionally, or just as part of your spiritual practice, the tools of Reiki II will assist you in becoming more centered, grounded, and open to the divine flow of energy all around us. While a simple practice, there is much to learn –not just in terms of knowledge and specific practices – but from the energy itself. It is easy to get caught up in the specifics of form, but Reiki offers us a means to move beyond form and into the formless bliss of that which we might call God Herself. Wherever this path takes you it is my wish that you follow your heart. May it lead you ever toward that great shining light of open-hearted consciousness.

Great and shining light
Descending from the heavens
One within my heart.

Appendix: Recommended Resources

Included here are some resources to help you get started in your Reiki practice, including some business resources that you may find to be helpful. While certainly not an exhaustive list there is enough here to get you started on the next phase of your journey.

Books

- *The Spirit of Reiki*
  by Walter Lübeck, Frank Arjava Petter, and William Rand

- *Magic of Reiki*
  by Christopher Penczak

- *Hands of Light*
  by Barbara Brennan

- *The Big Book of Reiki Symbols*
  by Mark Hosak and Walter Lübeck

- *Awakening the BlueLotus : A Reiki Level One Handbook*
  by Storm Faerywolf

Music

- *Reiki Gold: The Ultimate Reiki Album, Vol. 2*

- *Reiki River* by Niall

- *Celestial Reiki* by Jonathan Goldman & Laraaji

Websites

- James Deacon's Reiki Pages
  www.aetw.org

- International Center for Reiki Training
  www.reiki.org

- The Reiki Page (Information and directory of practitioners)
  www.reiki.7gen.com

Equipment for Sale

- Reiki Web Store
  www.reikiwebstore.com

- Massage Tools
  www.massage-tools.com

Business Cards

- www.VistaPrint.com

Web Design Tools

- Domain Registration:
    - GoDaddy.com
    - Register.com

Other projects by Storm Faerywolf:

The Mystic Dream is my online store. Visit TheMysticDream.com for more information and to peruse our books, crystals, and handmade spiritual and magical products.

Our online school offers long-distant and downloadable classes in various spiritual and magical modalities including Black Rose Witchcraft, Modern Conjure, Spiritual Cleansing, BlueLotus Reiki, and more! Visit www.TheMysticDreamAcademy.com for more info.

I am also a regular contributor to Modern Witch, a website, blog, and podcast. Check out www.ModernWitch.com.

Signed copies of my books can be purchased from www.TheMysticDream.com:

The Stars Within the Earth

Betwixt & Between: Exploring the Faery Tradition of Witchcraft

Forbidden Mysteries of Faery Witchcraft

Awakening the BlueLotus: A Reiki Level One Handbook

Becoming the BlueLotus: A Reiki Level Two Handbook

Mastering the BlueLotus: A Reiki Master/Teacher Handbook

Any additional projects will be listed on my website as they become available. www.faerywolf.com

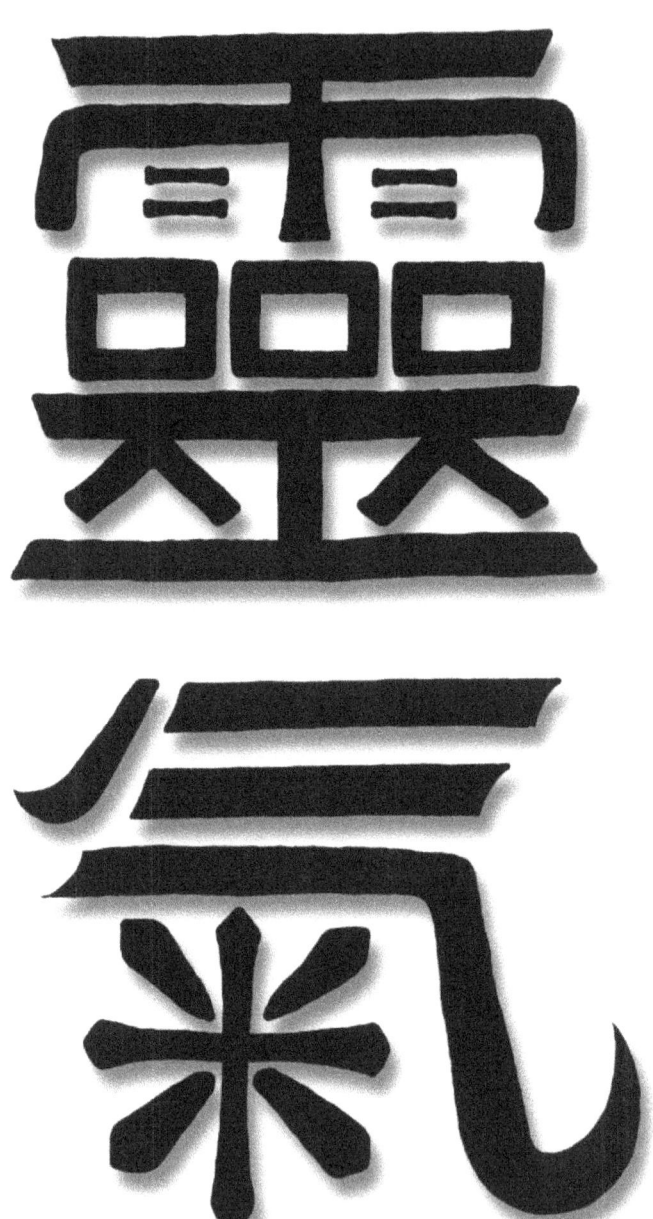

www.ingramcontent.com/pod-product-compliance
Lightning Source LLC
Chambersburg PA
CBHW031209090426
42736CB00009B/855